An Iron Shoes production
in association with the Unicorn

MAD ABOUT THE BOY

by Gbolahan Obisesan

MAD ABOUT THE BOY

by Gbolahan Obisesan

Boy	**Bayo Gbadamosi**
Dad	**Jason Barnett**
Man	**Simon Darwen**

Director	**Ria Parry**
Designer	**James Button**
Lighting Designer	**David W Kidd**
Sound Designer	**John Hoggarth**
Associate Director	**Laura Keefe**

Associate Producer	**Racheli Sternberg**
Press Manager	**Philip Strafford**
Production Manager	**Elaine Yeung**
Tour Publicity Designer	**Ned Glasier**

Mad About The Boy was developed with the support of the National Theatre Studio and ScenePool

Cast

Bayo Gbadamosi (*Boy*)
Theatre includes *Uncle Vanya* (parallel production); *The Litter, The Gods Are Not To Blame* (Young Vic); *Little Baby Jesus* (Ovalhouse); *The Brothers Size, Death of an Anarchist* (Dunraven Sixth Form).

Film includes *The Swarm* (Stray Bear); *Mission London* (Fidelity Films).

Jason Barnett (*Dad*)
Theatre includes the award-winning *Mogadishu* (Lyric Hammersmith/ Manchester Royal Exchange/tour); *Party Time/One for the Road* (BAC; JMK Award winner); *Jason and the Argonauts, The World Cup of 1966, Project D: I'm Mediocre* (BAC); *Julius Caesar, Burn* (Synergy Theatre Project); *The Fixer* (Almeida); *Come Out Eli* (tour; Time Out Award for Best New Production); *Winged* (Tristan Bates Theatre); *Cruising* (Bush); *A Midsummer Night's Dream, All the Right People Come Here* (Wimbledon Theatre); *The Victorian in the Wall, The Girlfriend Experience* (Royal Court); *Days of Significance, Pericles, The Winter's Tale* (Royal Shakespeare Company); *Amato Saltone* (National Theatre/Shunt); the multi award-winning original cast of *War Horse* (National Theatre).

Film includes *Rains of Fear, One Man and his Dog, Plotless, The Refugee*.

Television includes *Bad Education, Little Britain, Extras, The Sight, Dead Ringers, Coming of Age, Fur TV, Stupid!, The Slammer, Hotel Trubble, Vivien Vyle, The Legend of Dick and Dom, Doctors, The Bill* (Best Newcomer – Screen Nation Nomination 2008, RTS, BAFTA-winning ensemble 2009).

Simon Darwen (*Man*)
Theatre includes *The Taming of the Shrew* (Southwark Playhouse); *Love Love Love* by Mike Bartlett (Paines Plough/Drum Theatre Plymouth/national tour); *Unrestless* by Ben Ellis (Old Vic Tunnels); *Accolade* (Finborough); *Ramshackle Heart* (Public Theatre, New York); *Arse* by Colin Teevan, *Shove* (Theatre503), *Mad Forest* by Caryl Churchill, *The Wonder: A Woman Keeps a Secret* (BAC); *Jonny Macabe* (Arcola); *The Merchant of Venice, The Tragedy of Thomas Hobbes* by Adriano Shaplin, *The Taming of the Shrew, A Midsummer Night's Dream* (Royal Shakespeare Company); *Signs of Rust* by Ben Ellis, *1 in 5* by Penny Skinner (Hampstead); *Fanny & Faggot* by Jack Thorne (Finborough/ Trafalgar Studios); *Flamingos* by Duncan Macmillan, *Bedtime for Bastards* (nabokov); *24 Hour Plays: Ready* by Joel Horwood (Old Vic); *Romance, The Strange Case of Donovan Ray* both by Al Smith (Old Vic New Voices); *Nikolina* (nabokov/Theatre Royal Bath).

Film, television and radio includes *The Bill, Morris: A Life With Bells On, A Simple Man, Howard Everyman, Mayfly, Ready*.

Creative Team

Gbolahan Obisesan (Writer)
Gbolahan is a director and playwright. He was the recipient of the Bulldog Prinsep Bursary as Resident Director at the National Theatre Studio 2008/2009. In 2009 Gbolahan also won the Jerwood Directors' Award at the Young Vic Theatre for which he directed the critically acclaimed *SUS* by Barrie Keefe.

Other directing includes *Sixty-Six Books* (Bush); *Songs Inside* (Gate/ATC New Year's Revolution); *SUS* (national tour/Young Vic/Eclipse; Jerwood Directors' Award), *Eye/Balls*, *Hold it Up* (Soho); *200 years* (Watford Palace Theatre).

Writing includes *Mad About The Boy* (2011 Edinburgh Fringe First Award); *Set Me Fair – A May Fling* (Pentabus/Latitude); *Sweet Mother*, *Regeneration*, *A Vision of Pride* (Golden Delilah/Theatre503); *Deconstructing the Barack*, *Home* (Offstage Theatre, site specific at St Catherine's Tower, Leyton) and *Hold it Up* (National Youth Theatre/Soho).

Assistant directing includes *The Comedy of Errors*, *Fela!*, *Death and the King's Horseman* (for the Olivier Theatre at the National Theatre); *Alaska*, *random* (for the Royal Court); *Impempe Yomlingo* (for the Young Vic/Duke of York's; winner of an Olivier Award); *generations*, *Elsewhere: Heat & Light* (Hampstead); *The Astronauts Wives' Club* (Soho).

Ria Parry (Director)
Ria Parry is Co-Artistic Director of Iron Shoes. She received the Leverhulme Director's Bursary in 2010–11, becoming Director-in-Residence at the National Theatre Studio. Directing includes *Mad About The Boy* by Gbolahan Obisesan (Edinburgh Festival/national tour); *Fen* by Caryl Churchill (Finborough); *Rewind* (a devised production made in collaboration with young refugees and asylum seekers), and a young people's production of *King Lear* (Young Vic); *Our Hearts in the Balance* (British Museum); *Crush* by Paul Charlton (Edinburgh Festival/national tour). For Box Clever Theatre she has directed tours of *Romeo and Juliet*, *The Tempest*, *The Hate Play* and *The Buzz*. Ria was previously a Creative Producer at Watford Palace Theatre, and a member of the first Step Change Cultural Leadership Programme.

James Button (Designer)
James studied Theatre Design at Wimbledon School of Art. As an associate of Iron Shoes he has also designed *Fen* by Caryl Churchill (Finborough). Recent designs for theatre include *Orpheus and Eurydice* by Molly Davies and *Our Days of Rage* by Paul Roseby (Old Vic Tunnels); *The Trial*, *Gulliver's Travels* and *Grimm Tales* (Watford Palace Theatre); *Relish* by James Graham (Tramshed); *Living the Dream* by Joel Scott (World Expo 2010, Shanghai); *Rewind* and *King Lear* (Young Vic). Design for opera and dance include *The Strauss Gala*, choreographed by Christopher Hampson (Barbican Theatre/tour); *The Savage* by Jennifer Toksvig (Arcola Youth Opera). Film includes costume design for *Watch Over Me* (series 4) directed by Chris Jupe, and *Spiralling*, a short film directed by Nick Hillel. Forthcoming productions include *The Seed* by Goat & Monkey, and designer of the Welcoming Ceremonies at the 2012 Olympic Games.

David W Kidd (Lighting Designer)
David is an international lighting designer working in theatre, dance, ballet and opera. Recent dance productions include *Absent Made Present* (New Commissions for ROH2 Linbury, Royal Opera House); *Peter and the Wolf* (European/UK tour/New York); *Secret Garden Ballets* (Hatch House, Somerset); and Andersen's *Fairy Tales* (Bulgarian National Ballet). Opera includes *Die Walküre* (Denmark) and both Monserrat Caballé and Joan Sutherland in concert at Drury Lane. Previous work with Ria Parry and James Button includes *Fen* (Finborough); *Milestones* (Watford Palace Theatre); *Rewind* and *King Lear* (Young Vic). His extensive theatre credits in UK, Europe, Off-Broadway and London's West End include *Bully Boy*, *Little Eyolf*, *The River Line*, Woody Allen's *Writer's Block*, *The House of Bernarda Alba*, *Unsuspecting Susan*, *A Tribute to Ziegfried and Roy*, *Paul Merton Live!* at the Palladium, *The Anniversary*, *The Female Odd Couple*, *She Stoops to Conquer*, *Three Sisters* (2002 TMA Award Best Design) and *Reunion*. David lights the pantomimes at the Hackney Empire Theatre, most recently *Cinderella*.

John Hoggarth (Sound Designer)

John Hoggarth is Co-Artistic Director of Iron Shoes and was born and brought up in Whitby, North Yorkshire. He worked as an actor for several years before expanding his work to include writing and directing. In 2003 he became Joint Artistic Director of the National Youth Theatre and for several years combined the artistic directorship of the NYT with a prolific writing career. He moved on from the NYT in 2008 and in recent years has had his writing produced for television, radio and the stage. John has also developed a reputation for developing burgeoning comedy talent and has seen recent collaborations lead to a Perrier nomination, and the winning of both 'So Think You're Funny?' and the BBC new talent award. John co-wrote and directed the sketch show *The Ginge, The Geordie and The Geek* which had sell-out runs at the 2010 and 2011 Edinburgh Festival; the same team were commissioned by the BBC and completed a pilot episode of their sketch show in April 2012.

Laura Keefe (Associate Director)

Laura is an Iron Shoes Company Associate. Directing includes *The Forum* (Underbelly, Edinburgh); *I Know Where the Dead are Buried* and *The Fading Hum* (24/7 Theatre Festival, Manchester); *Miniaturists* (Arcola); *24 Hour Plays* (Old Vic New Voices); *Present : Tense* (nabokov). Comedy includes *Guilt and Shame* (Soho/Latitude/Edinburgh Festival/Bestival); *Checkley and Bush* (Latitude/Edinburgh Festival). Associate and assistant directing includes *Is Everyone OK?* (*nabokov*); *A Midsummer Night's Dream* (Regent's Park Open Air Theatre); *Salt, Root and Roe* (Donmar Warehouse/Trafalgar Studio 2); *Celebrity 24 Hour Plays* (Old Vic); *The Two Gentlemen of Verona* (Royal & Derngate, Northampton); *Fen* (Finborough/National Theatre Studio); *Doctor Faustus* (Watford Palace Theatre); *Romeo and Juliet* (Shakespeare's Globe); *Roaring Trade* (Soho/Paines Plough); *How to Disappear Completely and Never be Found* (Southwark Playhouse).

Racheli Sternberg (Associate Producer)

As an Iron Shoes Company Associate, Racheli was the Associate Producer on Caryl Churchill's *Fen* (Finborough). She has worked for the National Theatre at the Directors' Office, Studio and as an Assistant Producer on *War Horse* (New London Theatre and Lincoln Center Theater).

Philip Strafford (Press Manager)
Philip has worked in theatre PR for over ten years, having previously been Press Officer for the West Yorkshire Playhouse and Senior Press Officer for Sheffield Theatres. He moved into the world of freelancing in 2011 and now runs Pip-PR, a freelance agency, with a number of different clients he manages the media and public relations for a range of theatre, touring and arts companies. Philip also works part time as the publicist for the Department of Town and Regional Planning at the University of Sheffield.

Elaine Yeung (Production Manager)
Elaine trained in Professional Production Skills at Guildford School of Acting. Credits include *All the Fun of the Fair* (national tour); *Aladdin, Robinson Crusoe and the Caribbean Pirates* (SECC Glasgow, Qdos Entertainment); *Sandi Toksvig's Christmas Cracker* (Royal Festival Hall); *Francesca de Rimini, Rigoletto* (Opera Holland Park); *Time of My Life* (Watford Palace Theatre); *Death and the Maiden* (Salisbury Playhouse). Elaine first worked with Iron Shoes on their award-winning production *Crush* in Edinburgh Festival and on a national tour. Elaine is proud to be an Iron Shoes Company Associate and delighted to be Production Manager on *Mad About The Boy*.

Ned Glasier (Tour Publicity Designer)
Ned Glasier is a theatre director and occasional print designer and photographer. He is the artistic director of Islington Community Theatre and has directed plays and projects across the UK. He has designed publicity material for a wide range of London theatre companies. www.papersatellite.com

Special Thanks
Michael Ager, Carl Chambers, Phil Clarke, Anneliese Davidsen, Omar Elerian, Sue Emmas, Jessica Harwood, Kerry Irvine, Valmar Kass, Slavik Kirichok, David Lan, Richard Lee, Simon Manyonda, Lucy Maycock, Purni Morell, Diana Mumbi, Frederica Notley, Cyril Nri, Sarah Nicholson, Andy Shewan, Rachel Tyson, Jonathan Warde, West Yorkshire Playhouse, Janet Williamson, Madani Younis, and everyone at the Jerwood Space.

Tour Dates – 2012

Unicorn Theatre, London	12–19 May
Bush Theatre, London	28 May–2 June
Young Vic, London	6–16 June
The North Wall, Oxford	19–20 June
The Milton Rooms, Malton	25 June
Contact, Manchester	26–28 June
The Lantern Theatre, Sheffield	29 June
Rosehill Theatre, Cumbria	30 June
Bristol Old Vic, Bristol	27–29 September

Mad About The Boy was first performed in 2011 with the following casts:

Underbelly, Edinburgh Festival Fringe

Boy	**Bayo Gbadamosi**
Dad	**Cyril Nri**
Man	**Jamie Michie**

Transform Festival, West Yorkshire Playhouse

Boy	**Tosin Cole**
Dad	**Cyril Nri**
Man	**Gary Shelford**

Iron Shoes is a production company formed by John Hoggarth and Ria Parry. Iron Shoes is an Associate Company at the Bush Theatre.

Iron Shoes is dedicated to making quality theatre that is engaging, honest and accessible. Their first production, *Crush* by Paul Charlton, premiered at the Edinburgh Festival Fringe 2009, winning a Scotsman Fringe First Award. The production was also nominated for two Stage Awards and shortlisted for the Carol Tambor New York Award.

In 2010 they toured *Crush* around the UK, and worked with Kids Taskforce to create *Watch Over Me* (series 4), a television education drama written by John Hoggarth, delivered to secondary schools across the country in partnership with the Home Office.

In 2011 **Iron Shoes** produced *Fen* by Caryl Churchill in association with the National Theatre Studio and the Finborough Theatre. They co-produced *Surfing Tommies* by Alan Kent at the Minack Theatre, followed by a national tour in collaboration with BishBashBosh Productions. Their production of *Mad About The Boy* by Gbolahan Obisesan won a Scotsman Fringe First Award and was shortlisted for the Carol Tambor New York Award.

In 2012 **Iron Shoes** produced a UK tour of *Mad About The Boy* in association with the Unicorn.

Co-Artistic Directors: **John Hoggarth** and **Ria Parry**

Company Associates: **James Button, Paul Charlton, Claire Dargo, Neil Grainger, Kerry Irvine, Laura Keefe, David W Kidd, Racheli Sternberg, Elaine Yeung, BishBashBosh Productions**

Iron Shoes
Limber View, Glasidale,Whitby
North Yorkshire YO21 2QU
ironshoesproductions@me.com
www.ironshoes.co.uk

UNICORN Theatre for people under 21

The Unicorn Theatre is the largest theatre for young audiences in the UK. Founded in 1947 by Caryl Jenner, the company originally operated out of the back of a van, and pioneered bringing theatre for children into schools and community centres. The Unicorn was subsequently based at the Arts Theatre in London's West End for many years, before moving into its current home at London Bridge in 2005. Today, the Unicorn building has two theatres, two rehearsal rooms and four floors of public space dedicated to producing and presenting work for audiences aged two to twenty-one.

As an Arts Council National Portfolio Organisation, the Unicorn serves over 50,000 children, young people and families every year through its performances, youth theatre and other events. It is a central part of the theatre's mission to commission new work, to tour, to be accessible to all and to encourage exchange between theatre-makers from different countries and traditions to come together to develop ideas and projects.

For more information, visit **www.unicorntheatre.com**

Who We Are

Artistic Director
Purni Morell
Executive Director
Anneliese Davidsen
Finance Manager
Amanda Koch-Schick
Programme Producer
Carolyn Forsyth
Learning Associate
Catherine Greenwood
Youth Theatre Leader
Ruth Weyman
General Administrator
Jenny Skene

Technical Director
Phil Clarke
Technician (Sound)
Keith Edgehill
Technician (Lighting)
Shane Burke
Technician (Stages)
Jeff Mitchell
Technical Stage Manager
Andy Shewan
Building Technician
Martin Turner

Stage Door
Sidonie Ferguson & Alice Malseed

Director of Communications and Marketing
Nicki Marsh
Access Manager
Kirsty Hoyle

Marketing Coordinator
Isabel Madgwick
Schools Relationship Manager
Ella Macfadyen
Front of House Manager
Sair Smith
Box Office Manager
Helen Corbett

Director of Development
Dorcas Morgan
**Development Manager
(Trusts & Foundations)**
Caroline Darke (maternity cover)
**Development Manager
(Corporate & Individuals)**
Alexandra Jones
Development Officer
Melissa Wilkins

Front of House team
Lewis Church, Joycelyn Chung, Laura Fiesco, Clare Quinn, Clarrie Bent, Euan Borland, Geneva Corlett, Henry Reynolds, Housni Hassan, Jackie Downer, Katherine Tighe, Krystal Boyd-Maynard, Laura Standen, Lyn Medcalfe, Martin Walsh, Matthew Newell, Nadia Giscir, Nathan Rumney, Philip Moore, Robert Weaver, Stephanie Reed, Tom Dancaster, Martin Walsh, Christopher MacAllister

Box Office team
Laura Fiesco, Amy Mulholland, Claire Sundin, Julia Hayes, Euan Borland, Clare Quinn, Martin Walsh, Nadia Giscir

Board Giles Havergal, Denise Holle, Joanna Kennedy (Chair), Carolyn Maddox, Paul Meyer, Richard Oldfield, Bryan Savery, Keith Sharp, Sarah West

Youth Board Daniel Curthoys, Florence Dessau, Gabriella Jegede, Natalie Nelson, Maria Ratsevits, Liz Settimba, Kianna Witter-Prendergast, Douglas Wood

Supported using public funding by
**ARTS COUNCIL
ENGLAND**

Charity number: 225751
Company number: 480920

MAD ABOUT THE BOY

Gbolahan Obisesan

Acknowledgements

Thanks to Iron Shoes joint artistic directors John and Ria for their wholehearted commitment and dedication to the play from the very beginning. Thanks to the National Theatre Studio for the space for us to give it first breath. Thanks to all those that have helped to develop and produce the play and given the characters the vivid life that they deserve. Thanks to various friends and mentors who have always encouraged my writing, believing that this day will eventually come. Sorry to Mr Fox, Mr Camplin and a few other teachers – we should have been a bit more respectful in your classes. This play is for all the Boys that I know and many that I pass in the street. Boys who have tried or are still navigating the pressures and challenges of an inner-city comprehensive school. It's a difficult test. But you don't have to firm everything.

This play started with my father – he was a noble man who was mad at me, mad for me and more importantly truly mad about me. The only man I will forever be always mad about. R.I.P. N.O.A. Obisesan. Stay blessed.

Author's Note

The story is written in the Boy's vernacular, which is a distinct inner-city, post-modern language. It also represents the growing generational communications divide in most modern western societies.

The Man can be from an educated, working-class social background, or if cast with a regional accent, it should only be slightly distinct from that of the Boy.

The Dad should have a slight migrant's accent.

The staging should be bare, apart from the actors. The stage lighting should be minimal and sound should be used only where necessary and without lyrics.

Actors should ideally be facing the audience throughout the play. The director should use their artistic discretion to adhere to these instructions or not, based on having a clear alternative vision that will also best serve the storytelling.

Characters

BOY, *fourteen, must be this age or must without contention resemble this age; black/mixed race/Asian*

DAD, *mid- to late-forties, ethnicity must correlate to that of the Boy; if the Boy is cast as mixed-race, the Dad's ethnicity must be opposite to that of the Man*

MAN, *late-twenties/early-thirties, distinctly older than the Boy, but he should look significantly younger than the Dad; white/Asian/black/mixed-race*

Notes on Text

Words of dialogue in square brackets [ ] can either be said or omitted.

A dash (–) indicates an interruption or change in thought/intention in dialogue.

A forward slash (/) indicates an interruption by another character so that lines might overlap.

An ellipsis (…) indicates a trailing off of thought or a delayed response.

This text went to press before the end of rehearsals and so may differ slightly from the play as performed.

Scene One

DAD. My generation

MAN. Our generation

BOY. My generation

DAD. My generation had respect

MAN. Our generation gave respect

BOY. My generation wants respect

DAD. Respect was a thing you earned

MAN. respect was a thing you sought

BOY. respect is a thing you demand

DAD. demands were made by the community

MAN. demands were made by our parents

BOY. demand and if not given take it

DAD. It was our place to follow the rules

MAN. It was our place to bend the rules

BOY. it's our place to break the rules

DAD. Rules were made by the law

MAN. Rules were made for our benefit

BOY. Rules restrict our movements

DAD. Movements were against the law

MAN. Movements were to question the law

BOY. our movements are underground unknown by the law

DAD. Law and order was valued

MAN. Law dictated over our disorder

BOY. Law of disorder is the only way

DAD. Our generation toed the line

MAN. My generation tested the line

BOY. My generation cross the line

DAD. The line was compulsory

BOY. What line?

MAN. Compulsory to our development

BOY. What line?

DAD. In the army there's a line

BOY. My army's in the hood –

MAN. Your army's a lie

BOY. Can't lie to get into my army

DAD. Who's your enemy?

BOY. Everybody –

MAN. Your army are hoods

DAD. Hoods with no plans

BOY. Our plans run the hoods

MAN. Plans make the man

BOY. Manz have plans

DAD. Plans like what

MAN. what are your plans?

BOY. Plans to be top shotter?

DAD. Shotter?

BOY. Top shotter –

MAN. Top shotter?

BOY. Shotters makes P's

DAD. Peas?

BOY. P's –

MAN. Paper –

BOY. Don't act like –

MAN. Don't act like?

BOY. Like you know –

MAN. What?

BOY. Wong – Cheddar – Cream –

MAN. Money –

BOY. Money – like a banker

MAN. Banker?

BOY. Banker.

DAD. He wants to be a banker.

MAN. I don't think he wants to be a banker.

DAD. Bankers make money.

BOY. I wanna be money banking –

MAN. Money banking?

BOY. Banking money –

DAD. There banking money – bankers make and bank money –

MAN. money to a shotter is like banking.

BOY. There – It's like banking.

MAN. But it's not banking

DAD. It's not?

BOY. Why's it not?

DAD. Why not?

MAN. Why? – Cos – it's shotting.

BOY. Shotting – Banking – Slanging – slang.

DAD. for?

BOY. Slang for –

MAN. For people that hang around street corners –

BOY. Slinging –

DAD. Slinging?

BOY. Shotting –

MAN. Shotting – God knows what.

DAD. You want to be a slinger.

BOY. Slingers are everywhere –

DAD. everywhere?

MAN. everywhere there are slingers you find guns

DAD. guns?

MAN. Slingers carry guns –

DAD. Gunslingers!

MAN. Modern-day cowboys –

DAD. Cowboys like…?

BOY. Like Securicor guards protecting the banker's money

MAN. It's not the same.

BOY. It's so the same –

DAD. Is it the same?

MAN. Same lie, same difference –

BOY. Same then –

MAN. Can't say it's the same –

DAD. It's not the same – ?

BOY. It's the same –

MAN. as child soldiers fighting a civil war?

DAD. Fighting? – Civil war?

MAN. On the streets.

DAD. On the streets – ?

MAN. In our streets –

DAD. of course – the streets –

MAN. Our streets have become their new battlegrounds

BOY. Battlegrounds require live rounds –

DAD. You mean we live around –

BOY. It's just around –

DAD. Around where?

MAN. It's all around –

BOY. Don't mess around –

MAN. Who's messing around –

DAD. Leaving a mess –

MAN. It's a mess –

BOY. Mess you up –

DAD. Upside-down mess –

MAN. Gangs everywhere –

BOY. It's just code –

MAN. Postcode gangs –

DAD. Gang of boys – all colours – I've seen them

MAN. Seen them scheming – plotting –

BOY. What's your scheme – ?

MAN. who's scheming – ?

BOY. like you know – a plot can just be

MAN. just be – ?

BOY. also be where we – peeps – hang out

DAD. Hang out – no child of mine will be found hanging out

BOY. I ain't a child –

DAD. child… soldiers – as if –

MAN. fighting for rebels against the state system –

BOY. The system has failed –

MAN. The system hasn't failed

DAD. I feel the system might be failing these children –

MAN. These children are failing themselves –

DAD. you're failing them –

MAN. I'm not failing them – him –

DAD. They feel they are in a war against –

MAN. They are not in a war –

BOY. In a war you have to capitalise on every advantage –

MAN. Capitalise on every advantage –

BOY. Every advantage is a capitalist opportunity

DAD. No opportunity puts them at an advantage –

MAN. An advantage has to be seized

BOY. Seized not given –

MAN. Given to those that deserve it –

BOY. Deserve it – what I don't deserve it?

DAD. You don't think he deserves it?

MAN. I didn't say that.

BOY. You didn't say that, but you meant it.

DAD. Did you mean it?

MAN. I can't say that –

BOY. You meant it –

MAN. If you say so

BOY. I do say so

DAD. Don't be rude.

MAN. He's angry –

DAD. I should be angry –

BOY. I ain't angry –

MAN. You ain't angry?

DAD. Should be mad –

MAN. This is mad –

BOY. I'm not mad –

MAN. I didn't say –

DAD. He's not mad –

MAN. I didn't say – said –

BOY. Said mad – mad like how?

MAN. I didn't say –

DAD. How's he mad?

MAN. I didn't say –

BOY. Can't be mad.

DAD. He has ambition.

MAN. He's ambitious – Yes.

BOY. I've got ambition.

MAN. ambition to be…?

BOY. to be…

MAN. Bad?

DAD. What do you mean bad?

MAN. It had to be said –

BOY. Bad – (*Thinking*.)

DAD. He ain't bad –

BOY. Ambitiously bad ain't bad –

DAD. It's bad to plant that sort of –

MAN. I ain't planting –

BOY. who's plant – what?

DAD. He's just a kid –

MAN. Just a kid –

DAD. A kind kid.

MAN. Yep… Kind –

BOY. Kinda bad

DAD. Bad to think –

MAN. It's bad –

BOY. *Baaad maaan* –

DAD. Listen, man – he's keen –

MAN. Keen to…?

DAD. Keen as any other –

MAN. Others aren't keen –

DAD. Keen on?

BOY. ain't no keeno –

MAN. Keen to –

DAD. He's still keen to –

BOY. Keener than others to –

MAN. to learn?

BOY. to learn – ?

DAD. that's my point –

BOY. what's the –

MAN. Point taken –

DAD. He's not bad then –

MAN. He's not bad.

BOY. Keen to be bad.

DAD. I didn't bring him up to be bad.

BOY. I'm just bad.

DAD. Shut up –

MAN. Bad to shout [it] –

DAD. I'm his dad.

MAN. Yes… Dad – you must see.

BOY. See my dad.

MAN. you must see.

DAD. I must see.

BOY. see my dad –

MAN. See your –

DAD. See what?

MAN. He's turning bad.

DAD. Turning bad?

BOY. Turning bad?

MAN. You're turning bad –

DAD. Turning bad how?

BOY. How am I turning bad?

MAN. Changes –

BOY. Changes?

MAN. I've seen changes in –

DAD. Changes how?

BOY. How are there changes?

MAN. Changes how you – we look at you.

BOY. Look at me?

DAD. Look at me –

MAN. Look at me –

BOY (*mockingly*). Look at me –

MAN. We look at you –

BOY. You look at me…?

DAD. Look at him –

MAN. Differently –

DAD. Differently?

BOY. How differently?

DAD. How differently?

MAN. Differently like you need help.

BOY. Like I need help?

DAD. Like I need help.

MAN. Yes –

DAD. I know the help he needs.

MAN. I know the help you need.

BOY. You know the help I need.

DAD. Know the help we need.

BOY. What helps that then?

MAN. Help that's…

DAD. No help –

MAN. No help?

BOY. No help.

MAN. Just a little help.

DAD. A little help is too much

BOY. Too much already – A little help is too much.

MAN. It doesn't have to be too much.

DAD. It's already too much – you've said too much.

BOY. Too much.

MAN. I didn't mean –

DAD. You didn't mean?

MAN. I mean sorry – If you felt

DAD. I felt –

MAN. I didn't mean to make you feel –

DAD. You made me feel –

BOY. Made manz feel – You make us feel –

MAN. Trying to make you feel –

DAD. I don't want you to make me feel –

BOY. We don't want you to –

DAD. I'm his dad.

MAN. I see you're his dad.

DAD. I am his dad.

MAN. Dad, he's –

BOY. a bad man

MAN. a… bad boy

DAD. Bad boy?

BOY. I'm a bad man.

MAN. Badman?

BOY. Yes bad man –

MAN. What'd you mean bad man?

DAD. What do you mean – ?

BOY. Mean don't give a shit.

MAN. Don't give a shit?

BOY. Don't give a shit.

DAD. I give a shit.

MAN. I give a shit.

BOY. Shit, ain't bad man.

MAN. Shit, ain't bad?

DAD. I ain't a bad man.

BOY. Ain't bad to be a bad man.

MAN. That's too bad.

BOY. Too bad?

MAN. just too bad.

BOY. Nah, how's it too bad.

MAN. You know –

BOY. No – what?

DAD. What's to know?

MAN. How to be good.

DAD. Be good?

MAN. Yes – Do good.

DAD. Do good?

BOY. I'm glad you –

DAD. Woh – he's not that bad.

MAN. he's not that bad.

BOY. Bad to the bone.

DAD. Shut up.

BOY. What?

MAN. That's what – Show him strength.

DAD. Show him strength?

MAN. You show him strength?

DAD. Strength like no other.

BOY. Strength to the bone.

DAD. Bone idle sometimes –

MAN. Sometimes in class –

BOY. Class is idle, but I'm still a class idol.

MAN. Idols have class –

BOY. That's what I'm saying.

DAD. Saying you're idle to the bone in class

BOY. Sometimes manz is idle to the bone and what.

DAD. What? – Pure self-idolatry

MAN. Lazy idolatry indeed –

BOY. Check my class – Peeps still worship my deeds –

DAD. deeds? – I'll give you deeds when we get home?

MAN. What – You smack him?

DAD. Smack him?

MAN. Yes smack him.

DAD. Smacking is –

MAN. Smacking.

BOY. Smacked it bare times.

DAD. Times have changed.

BOY. Change the record.

MAN. Records show bruises –

DAD. Bruised his ego more like –

MAN. More like from smacking –

DAD. Smacking is –

MAN. Smacking.

BOY. Smacked it like a bad man.

DAD. Shut up.

MAN. Man has to smack.

DAD. Smacking – man to man.

MAN. Man to man – Yes.

BOY. Smacked it better than a next man.

DAD. Smack you [in a minute] –

BOY. Smack me – [Nah].

MAN. *Yes…*

DAD. Most next men might smack –

MAN. Next men do smack.

DAD. Next men might smack –

BOY. Smack me? – nah – I ain't a next man –

MAN. *Next man?*

DAD. Next men might smack –

BOY. Smack a next man

MAN. Next man?

BOY. Next man can't touch me at smacking it

DAD. Smacking it's... Next man might smack – Smacking I think is no good.

BOY. No good at smacking it like I do.

MAN (*confidentially*). I do

DAD. Do you?

MAN. I do –

DAD. Good for you.

MAN. wouldn't it be good...?

BOY. Good to send you down

DAD. pipe down –

MAN. It's good for...

DAD. Breeding contempt.

BOY. What I do –

MAN. Breeds contempt?

DAD. Breeds contempt.

MAN. Breeds respect.

BOY. Breeds respect.

MAN. Respect has to be bred.

DAD. Doesn't breed respect, 'swhy I chose not to smack

MAN. If you do – smack – I won't [tell]

DAD. I don't – I'll be put away.

MAN. So what do you choose?

BOY. Choices are limited, 'swhy –

DAD. I choose to do good.

BOY. Good at smacking to the bone.

DAD. He's got a strong back.

BOY. I'm strongly backed

DAD. I'll back him through anything.

BOY. Anything and I'm backed –

MAN. Back against the wall – Must be hard.

BOY. Must be hard.

DAD. Hardens your skin.

BOY. Skin breda's for fun.

MAN. Can't be fun.

DAD. Funny you should say that –

MAN. Funny?

BOY. Funny (*Chuckles to himself.*)

DAD. Funny.

MAN. How's it funny?

DAD. Funny what he gets up to –

MAN. What he gets up to?

BOY. What I – we get up to?

MAN. What's funny about that?

BOY. Jokes (*Laughing to himself.*)

MAN. What's the joke?

DAD. Joking aside –

BOY (*condescending*). Bare jokes

MAN. Joking aside

DAD. aside from the trouble – I find it funny.

BOY. It's funny.

MAN. You find it funny.

BOY. Ha. Ha. Ha –

DAD. Hats off to him –

MAN. For punching a supply teacher –

BOY. Supply teachers are dumb –

DAD. Called him dumb –

MAN. Dumb doesn't excuse it –

DAD. It's not an excuse –

BOY. Excuse me for not dumbing down

MAN. It went down to the last vote –

DAD. Last vote –

BOY. It got the minority vote –

MAN. against the majority vote –

BOY. Class is full of minorities – take a photo of the class

MAN. Classic special case –

DAD. Special case –

BOY. Special cases like that teacher needed to be put in their
    place –

MAN. Places him in the ASBO category –

DAD. Category?

BOY. Try categorise me –

MAN. Anti-social behaviour order –

DAD. I know –

BOY. I know it was – but it felt good.

MAN. Felt good to have voted against sending him –

DAD. Sending him?

BOY. Sending him *faaalllling* – (*Illustrates punch on supply
    teacher.*)

MAN. To a pupils' referral unit –

DAD. Referral unit –

MAN. It's what the school – teachers' council wanted.

DAD. You did that –

BOY. I did that.

MAN. I did that –

DAD. That's unexpected –

BOY. Unexpected by everyone –

MAN. Everyone's had enough –

DAD. Had enough –

MAN. Of dealing with him

BOY. Dealt with him –

DAD. I'll deal with him.

MAN. With him – they want to wash their hands.

DAD. They can't wash their hands

BOY. Hands needed washing from the blood

DAD. Bloody teachers –

MAN. Bloody teachers –

BOY. Bloody teachers –

DAD. There must be something –

MAN. Something can always be done

BOY. Done what I had to

DAD. Too hard to think –

BOY. Now everyone thinks I'm too hard –

MAN. Hard to think –

BOY. Harder than before

MAN. Before the hard times –

DAD. Times are hard

BOY. Hard times require hard responses

DAD. He hardly responses – It's hard sometimes.

BOY. I'm hard – all the time.

MAN. Got to be hard.

DAD. Hard to deal with.

MAN. We could strike a deal with –

BOY. deal with the matter –

MAN. deal with it proper

DAD. what would a proper deal be?

MAN. It'll be a proper deal.

DAD. dealt with by who?

MAN. Whoever needs to be involved –

DAD. Involving other people?

BOY. People who aren't involved can step back –

MAN. Other people would have to be involved

DAD. what would they…?

MAN. They would –

DAD. They would – ?

MAN. Split –

DAD. Split what?

MAN. Split the two –

DAD. Split the two?

BOY. They can split –

DAD. Split for what?

BOY. Can't split me –

DAD. He'll be taken away…

MAN. Foster care

BOY. Foster care?

MAN. Foster care –

BOY. Are you drunk?

MAN. No –

BOY. Then don't take the piss –

MAN. I'm not trying to piss you off –

BOY. Like I care for fosters

DAD. Can't have him in foster care.

MAN. Foster care ain't so bad.

BOY. Ain't so bad?

DAD. shhh – ain't so bad?

BOY. Dad.

DAD.…

MAN. I was raised in foster care.

BOY. Foster care?

MAN. Foster care.

BOY. Explains it.

MAN. Explains what?

BOY. Your behaviour.

MAN. Behaviour?

DAD. Behaviour?

BOY. Hard on –

DAD. Hard on?

MAN. Hard on what?

BOY. Hard on us than teachers.

DAD. Isn't he your teacher.

MAN. Teachers are supposed to be hard.

BOY. Teachers ain't –

DAD. They're teachers – ?

MAN. They aren't.

BOY. A bit of a walkover.

DAD. Walkover?

BOY. Like a Persian rug.

MAN. Persian rug.

DAD. Jokers.

MAN. Scared.

BOY. Scared of what?

DAD. Scared of what?

MAN. Scared of complaints.

    BOY *laughs throughout underneath.*

DAD. Complaints?

MAN. Harassment.

DAD. Harassment?

MAN. Sexual.

DAD. Sexual?

MAN. Prejudice.

DAD. Prejudice.

MAN. Discrimination.

DAD. Discrimination?

MAN. Racism.

DAD. Racism?

MAN. They're not.

BOY (*stops laughing*). How do we know?

MAN. They're not.

DAD. How do we know?

BOY. We don't know –

MAN. They're not –

DAD. They're not?

MAN. They're not.

BOY. You say that –

MAN. That's the truth.

BOY. No one knows the truth.

DAD. There isn't an absolute truth.

MAN. truth can be absolute.

BOY. For you.

DAD. I don't want him in foster care –

    I'm here –

MAN. …you've just got to trust me.

BOY. I don't.

MAN. That's sad.

BOY. pussies are sad.

MAN. …

DAD. Don't say that

BOY. That's the truth.

MAN. Isn't it sad?

DAD. Sad?

MAN. to be sadly alone –

BOY. Who's [alone] ? – *pussies*. ain't. got. no. backing.

MAN. Back to the wall.

BOY. Getting jacked on their J's.

DAD. It's hard alone sometimes.

MAN. Sometimes I find it difficult

DAD. difficult to admit sometimes

MAN. It's about keeping up –

BOY (*demands*). Keep up.

MAN. Keeping up.

BOY. We – *I* ain't alone.

MAN. Struggling alone.

DAD. Struggling all the time.

BOY. Time you know man like me *ain't* about struggling.

DAD. It can't be helped.

BOY. I'm helping myself.

MAN. You don't have to do it yourself.

DAD. Do what?

MAN. Survive.

DAD. Me and the boy survive fine.

BOY. Boy – you don't know nothing about me.

MAN. Fine?

BOY. Know some people think I'm dangerous

MAN. Dangerous.

BOY. Yeah – as in hazardous to your health.

DAD. what?

MAN. How healthy is that?

BOY. Do I make you sick?

MAN. There's a danger.

DAD. Danger of what?

MAN. Of losing patience –

BOY. What's your complaint?

DAD. Complaining doesn't solve anything –

MAN. Anything can happen –

DAD. Like what?

BOY. Like what?

MAN. There's a risk –

DAD. Risk of what?

BOY. What's the risk?

MAN. Falling into the wrong hands.

BOY. *Wrooong!*

DAD. Hands?

MAN. I'm showing my hand –

BOY. What's your card?

MAN. This is an opportunity –

DAD. Depends on what cards you're dealt.

BOY. I've been dealt the upper hand – those are my cards.

MAN. Can't stack the odd –

DAD. The odds are –

BOY. The odds I stack

MAN. The odds are stacked –

BOY. I stack the odds

DAD. The odds are stacked in

BOY. In my favour

DAD. In our favour

MAN. Against –

BOY. I stack the odds

DAD. Against?

MAN. Against.

BOY. Against anyone that tries to test.

MAN. Against you both.

Scene Two

BOY. What do you know about girls?

MAN. What do I know – ?

BOY. About girls.

MAN. About girls?

BOY. You're not deaf.

MAN. I know I'm not deaf.

BOY. Then why are you carrying on like Beethoven –

MAN. I don't think I should – How do you know he was deaf?

BOY. Why? – Shouldn't I know?

MAN. It's not that you shouldn't know – just wondering how you do?

BOY. I just do.

MAN. You just do –

BOY. yeah –

MAN. Fine…

BOY. He went deaf in his twenties, but carried on making music –

MAN. That's right –

BOY. He felt it –

MAN. Definitely –

BOY. I like music you can feel –

MAN. Like?

BOY. Anything as long as I feel it –

MAN. Tell the girl –

BOY. what?

MAN. Tell her –

BOY. tell her I feel music –

MAN. Yeah – why not?

BOY. I want to feel her that's why –

MAN. She might be feeling you if you tell her something about yourself –

BOY. That's moist –

MAN. What's that?

BOY. It's weak – I ain't weak.

MAN. Stop being wet –

BOY. I'm trying to get her wet –

MAN. You got no respect –

BOY. and –

MAN. where's your respect?

BOY. What you talking about?

MAN. respect – ?

BOY. respect what?

MAN. Her, the girl –

BOY. why?

MAN. because you like her –

BOY. So?

MAN. So it's just nice –

BOY. But I'm not nice – I mean – I'm *nice* like buff, but not nice like spice –

MAN. girls like nice –

BOY. Not all girls like nice –

MAN. No not all girls –

BOY. So I'll go for the ones that don't like that nice –

MAN. no girl's never not liked nice –

BOY. This is confusing – what are you saying?

MAN. It's complicated –

BOY. why do you have to make it complicated – ?

MAN. Girls like – Women like nice and some *like* – as you say, prefer *nice* –

BOY. Buff nice –

MAN. Yeah, but some might not even be nice –

BOY. Ugly.

MAN. Yes – No – I mean – I meant – soft – hardened women

BOY. Hard women?

MAN. Yeah. Some hard women still like nice men

BOY. what like Peter Andre?

MAN. I don't know – maybe.

BOY. I ain't no Peter Andre though –

MAN. No?

BOY. Ain't. no. Peter. Andre. –

MAN. Okay you're not Peter Andre

BOY. As long as you know –

MAN. I know now –

BOY. You done know –

MAN. I know now you're not Peter Andre, but some women like that sort of nice and under the circumstances – this girl you like might be one of those types of women and if she's as nice as you've made her to be, she might also be a girl that's nice to other women –

BOY. lesbians –

MAN. Yes – which means they're not nice for you –

BOY. You mean I'm not nice to them –

MAN. Exactly – so they won't fancy you –

BOY. You think she's lesbian?

MAN. No I never said that –

BOY. But you're suggesting –

MAN. That not all girls are gonna like you –

BOY. Because they're lesbian –

MAN. No – probably because they don't think you're nice –

BOY. But I am nice –

MAN. Maybe not as nice to them as you might like –

BOY. Alright I hear that… but what if I find a nice girl that the lesbian thinks is nice and because the nice girl thinks I'm nice, the lesbian girl then starts to think uh actually he's quite nice and she wants me and the nice girl and her to nice up their sheets with all our wetness like one big paddling pool –

MAN. That might never happen –

BOY. Maybe not to you

MAN. You've got to be realistic.

BOY. but. what. if. it. did –

MAN. It's unlikely –

BOY. why's it unlikely?

MAN. because your nice girl might just go off with the other nice girl –

BOY. The lesbian –

MAN. the lesbian – because your nice girl thinks the other girl is nicer and no longer thinks you or guys are nice –

BOY. that's not nice though is it –

MAN. it's just the way things are sometimes –

BOY. I don't want sometime-ish – I want my bit whenever I want it –

MAN. we don't always get what we want when we want it –

BOY. You might not –

MAN. What does that mean?

BOY. Exactly what it is.

MAN. If I know I can't have it I forget about it –

BOY. That's waste –

MAN. Maybe –

BOY. You're a waste, man –

MAN. I don't know what you mean –

BOY. You've got no ambition – you're a giver-rup-per

MAN. I'm not –

BOY. Don't sound like it –

MAN. I understand what it sounds like, but that's not the reality –

BOY. so what's the reality?

MAN. It just. Sometimes we ain't always in control, but the bit that we are in control of we want it to run smoothly –

BOY. Do you think you're in control right now?

MAN. I'm trying to maintain control –

BOY. maintain – hold on to – you can't hold me.

MAN. You're obligated to be here –

BOY. Yeah, it's my school – why are you here?

MAN. I'm the school counsellor –

BOY. So what –

MAN. so what.

BOY. so what if you wasn't?

MAN. but I am, it's my job.

BOY. What if you wasn't – you had another job – the job you've always wanted…

MAN. another job?

BOY. You've always wanted…

MAN.…an artist –

BOY. what?

MAN. maybe an artist –

BOY. Artist?

MAN. Yes artist –

BOY. That's waste – they don't do shit –

MAN (*laughs*). You asked –

BOY. Politician!

MAN. don't make me laugh –

BOY. Just trying to give you more options – make you ambitious –

MAN. A politician?

BOY. Yeah you could be a good politician –

MAN. A good politician?

BOY. You like telling people what to do don't you –

MAN. It's not –

BOY. Look – If you want people to listen to you – you put them in their place – (*Gesturing with finger pointed downwards with attitude.*) and tell them what to do –

MAN. You like telling people what to do.

BOY. That's what I'm saying – I was born to tell people what to do –

MAN. So you could be a good politician.

BOY. Spending all that money on wars and holiday homes and shit like that – Hell yeah –

MAN. That's a bad politician –

BOY. Not if it's what I have to do –

MAN. You could find a better way – a better solution to the decisions you need to make –

BOY. What – Like – hide it from people?

MAN. That would make you a really bad politician –

BOY. But isn't that just being smart?

MAN. a smart politician would find the right way to do the job properly in the first place –

BOY. It don't matter anyway, they've let in Obama now so the door's shut for say fifty years –

MAN. President of America might not work anyway –

BOY. Why?

MAN. Cos you're not American – Prime Minister on the other hand –

BOY. That won't work either –

MAN. why not?

BOY. Do I look English?

MAN. That's not the correct attitude to have –

BOY. You're not a politician so you can't tell me what sort of attitude to have –

MAN. I've been placed here by our current best politicians to be your attitude-adjuster –

BOY. If you want me to adjust my attitude – tell me how to get the girl I like to give me head –

MAN. …If that's all you want her for, then why should she?

BOY. She should because she's a sket –

MAN. what?

BOY. a jezzie –

MAN. je– what?

BOY. Slit

MAN. Woh –

BOY. Cunt –

MAN. pardon –

BOY. Shinners –

MAN. Stop –

BOY. Knob polisher –

MAN. Can you –

BOY. Porridge pot –

MAN. Stop –

BOY. Spunk bucket –

MAN. that's enough –

BOY. waste basket –

MAN. THAT'S ENOUGH –

BOY. that's what I think –

MAN. You can't talk about –

BOY. what?

MAN. About women like that –

BOY. who says?

MAN. women – I say –

BOY. Like I care what anyone thinks –

MAN. What if someone spoke about your sister like that –

BOY. I ain't got no sister –

MAN. For the sake of argument –

BOY. I ain't arguing –

MAN. Then you've got a sister –

BOY. No I ain't –

MAN. This girl you're talking about – anyhow – she is your sister?

BOY. No she's not.

MAN. But what if she was?

BOY. But she's not –

MAN. she's not but she could be.

BOY. I don't see how she could be, because she's not

MAN. hypothetically –

BOY. Hypo– what?

MAN. Let's imagine – Let's suppose – let's imagine

BOY. Imagine what?

MAN. That this girl is you sister.

BOY. Why you saying that – why are you doing that?

MAN. If she was your sister –

BOY. she's not – stop it –

MAN. would you still like – Other boys talking –

BOY. why are you still talking?

MAN. look at her like –

BOY. Like man would fuck his own sister –

MAN. undressing her – doing – saying disrespectful –

BOY. disrespecting man's right to want woman –

MAN. misogyny – that's what it's called –

BOY. You must miss ogling –

MAN. Ogling?

BOY. I bet –

You must *like* ogling –

MAN. Ogling? – I don't do ogling –

BOY. Take a mental picture do you – Hold it in for your spank
bank?

MAN. what?

BOY. Tell me you don't spank – errh you spank.

MAN. I don't think that's appropriate –

BOY. I don't think what you're saying is appropriate.

MAN. what if she was your mother?

BOY. My mother's dead – I killed her.

MAN. What?

BOY. You heard –

MAN. What makes you think you killed her?

BOY. because I did –

MAN. How is that possible?

BOY. I ruptured her punani –

MAN. I don't understand?

BOY. I collapsed her pussy –

MAN. Is that a figure of speech?

BOY. That's what happened.

MAN. how could that have happened –

BOY. It just did.

MAN. To your own mother?

BOY. When she had me – she bled to death – Done.

MAN. I wish you wouldn't –

BOY. wouldn't tell the truth –

MAN. No – be so graphic

BOY. I'm a graphic maverick –

MAN. graphic maverick?

BOY. Larger-than-life rebel –

MAN. you revel in that don't you.

BOY. that's why people like me.

MAN. People don't like you – the girl doesn't like you.

BOY. chatting shit –

MAN. think about it –

BOY. why you saying that?

MAN. it's the truth.

BOY. I don't wanna hear that –

MAN. It's important –

BOY. Who's been talking foolishness?

MAN. It's not foolishness – you need to find out why they don't like you?

BOY. I need to know who they are, so I can kill them.

MAN.…Kill them?

BOY. Make their head trickle – slosh poppies –

MAN. let's not rush our thoughts – not make hasty conclusions

BOY. fuck this –

Scene Three

MAN. So tell me.

BOY. Tell you…

MAN. Tell me –

DAD. Tell us.

BOY. What?

DAD. What do you mean what.

MAN. What happened?

BOY. It happened.

DAD. Exactly –

MAN. How did it happen?

BOY. It just did.

DAD. Just did?

MAN. Things don't just happen.

BOY. Well this did.

DAD. You can't just –

MAN. So how did it start?

BOY. From the start?

MAN. From the start.

DAD. How it started.

BOY. Alright.

DAD. Right.

MAN. Alright – It's alright.

BOY. Don't patronise me –

MAN. Not trying to patronise you –

DAD. Don't try and get clever –

BOY. Clever?

DAD. This is serious.

BOY. Like I don't know –

MAN. Let's just get the –

DAD. Let's just – / go on then.

BOY. Has he got to –

DAD. Got to what?

MAN. Got to.

BOY. But he's –

DAD. I'm what?

MAN. Let's just –

DAD. Let's just – As if I ain't got enough on my plate.

BOY. You've always got something on your plate.

DAD. Who's plate am I trying to fill?

BOY. Fill my own plate –

DAD. Oh yeah?

BOY. Yeah.

MAN. Can we – ?

DAD. Is that right?

MAN. Can we – ?

BOY. That's right.

DAD. I'll hand my plate over to you more then –

MAN. We've all got enough on our plates

DAD. Don't tell me –

MAN. Please – both of you.

DAD. I ain't got a problem –

BOY. My problem ain't you –

DAD. What's that supposed to mean?

MAN. It doesn't mean anything.

BOY. If you can't take a guess.

DAD. Guess what?

BOY. I ain't saying what it means –

DAD. So it means nothing then?

BOY. I ain't saying that.

MAN. That's not what he's saying.

DAD. What's he saying then – you seem to understand him.

BOY. You don't understand me –

MAN. That's what he's saying.

DAD. …Saying that to me?

MAN. Unfortunately

DAD. Saying that to me.

MAN. I don't think he meant

BOY. I meant it –

MAN. I'm trying to help you.

BOY. I don't need any help.

DAD. He doesn't need any help – knows it all.

MAN. He doesn't know it all.

BOY. I don't know it all.

DAD. That's got to be a first.

BOY. 'Swhy she was helping me.

DAD. What?

MAN (*prompting*). Yes?

BOY. She helped me.

MAN. With?

BOY. My work.

DAD. You do work?

BOY. Yeah –

MAN. He does work.

DAD. He does work?

BOY. Work hard.

DAD. Works hard!?

BOY. When I want to.

DAD. When *he* wants to.

BOY. Bits that I get.

MAN. He does work – He's improved.

BOY. I improved cos she helped me –

DAD. So she was helping you –

MAN. she's been a good influence.

BOY. I didn't want her to at first –

MAN. You didn't want her to?

BOY. At first.

DAD. Too proud.

MAN. Too proud?

BOY. Get it from my dad.

DAD. I know what that feels like.

MAN. I know what that feels like.

BOY. Felt like man was weak –

MAN. It's not weak –

DAD. We're not weak.

BOY. I'm not weak

MAN. Was it every week –

BOY. Every week –

DAD. Days of the week –

BOY. Nearly every day – seeing her.

DAD. Seeing her?

MAN. Seeing her?

BOY. To go through schoolwork –

DAD. Schoolwork.

BOY. She was neeky.

DAD. Needy?

BOY. Neeky.

MAN. Nerdy and geeky –

DAD. Smart –

BOY. Bad combination –

MAN. Causes complications –

BOY. There were other complications –

DAD. Other complications?

BOY. She was on me.

DAD. She was on you?

MAN. On you – Harsh?

DAD. Was she harsh with you?

BOY. Nah – on me.

DAD. Yeah – she was harsh on you.

MAN. She flirted with you?

DAD. Flirt?

BOY. Nah – not exactly – not at first –

MAN. Not at first?

DAD. What happened at first?

BOY. She kept it quiet –

MAN. Quiet?

BOY. Yeah – you know – low-key.

DAD. Under the radar –

BOY. Something like that –

DAD. You didn't get an erection when you were with her.

MAN. Please –

DAD. I'm just saying – that's what he meant –

MAN. But –

BOY. He's right she wasn't exciting –

DAD. She wasn't exciting –

MAN. Not exciting?

BOY. She was expecting.

MAN. Expecting?

DAD. Expecting what?

BOY. I don't know?

MAN. You don't know?

DAD. You must know.

BOY. She's weird –

DAD. A weird girl –

MAN. She's peculiar –

BOY. Peculiar?

MAN. Strange.

BOY. Yeah – mad strange.

DAD. Strange girl –

BOY. but bang on it.

MAN. She liked you?

BOY. A lot.

DAD. The weird girl liked you a lot – that's strange.

BOY. That's what I thought.

MAN. Thought you got on?

BOY. recently – we started getting on.

DAD. Not getting it on.

BOY. Not getting it on.

MAN. But you got on.

BOY. She wanted to be Facebook friends?

DAD. I've heard about that –

MAN. and?

BOY. I ignored her –

MAN. You didn't accept her?

BOY. I didn't accept her.

MAN. Why not?

DAD. You know why not?

BOY. If people found out.

MAN. People?

DAD. People.

BOY. Peeps at school.

MAN. What does it matter?

BOY. It matters.

MAN. It shouldn't matter.

BOY. It shouldn't but that's just routine.

DAD. Routine?

BOY. You keep to your own –

DAD. Who's your own?

BOY. She's not my own.

MAN. She could be.

BOY. But she's not – it doesn't work like that.

MAN. How does it work?

BOY. She started sending me messages.

MAN. messages?

DAD. On Facebook

BOY. Nah – when I was with her.

MAN. When you were with her?

DAD. Like what?

BOY. You know.

DAD. What's to know?

BOY. Smelling nice –

MAN. Smelling nice?

BOY. Looking different –

DAD. Looking different?

BOY. Make-up – short skirt – big breast –

DAD. And –

MAN. And what else –

BOY. I…

DAD. yes?

BOY. I accidentally touched her knee

MAN. What happened?

BOY. She kept my hand there –

DAD. She kept his hand there – that says it all –

MAN. Is that all?

DAD. Was it all the time?

BOY. That's not all –

DAD. That's not all?

MAN. What else?

BOY. One time –

DAD. What time?

MAN. What time did things change?

BOY. About one month ago –

DAD. A month ago?

BOY. …She started letting me finger her.

DAD. What?

BOY. she'd get all hot down there – start rubbing my dick.

DAD. You were supposed to be studying –

BOY. I know –

DAD. See what girls do to young boys –

BOY. I'm not a boy –

DAD. Since the dawn of time –

BOY. Time man was known as a man –

DAD. Man has no chance –

MAN. Was that the only time?

BOY. Boy she started looking fine.

DAD. How fine? – what did you do?

MAN. what happened?

BOY (*boastful*). We started fucking?

DAD. fucking – What?

MAN. When?

BOY. After school – Around the school –

DAD. How's that allowed to go on?

MAN. It's –

BOY. No one knew?

DAD. No one knew – what kind of school is this.

MAN. It's –

BOY. I started swagging –

MAN. swagging?

BOY. Bouncing about everywhere – acting strange –

MAN. acting strange –

BOY. Being nice to people –

MAN. that's not so bad –

BOY. my batch started taking the piss

MAN. who started taking the piss

DAD. batch?

MAN. His friends –

BOY. They're not my friends –

DAD. You can't be friends with people that take the piss –

BOY. calling man a neek –

DAD. That's bad isn't it?

BOY. trying to oust me –

DAD. Oust what?

BOY. I ain't giving up without a fight –

MAN. You could have got out –

BOY. I *don't* want out –

MAN. You've got to lodge them at some point –

DAD. Become your own man –

BOY. I'm always my own man

DAD. doesn't sound like it –

BOY. What do you know?

DAD. Sounds like you're a sheep –

BOY. like you know

DAD. Can't stand for this –

MAN. Let's get to the – when did that stop?

BOY.…

DAD (*impatiently*). well – ?

MAN. please – what's changed?

BOY. They tried to rush me –

DAD. Why didn't you fight them?

BOY. They go too far – They would put me in hospital and think it's normal –

MAN. So what did you do?

BOY....I told them.

MAN. You told them –

DAD. what?

BOY. That my girl –

DAD. she's your girl –

BOY. Not my girl – just –

MAN. you said what?

BOY. that she's putting out –

DAD. Putting out –

MAN. You gave her up –

BOY. to get them off my back – She was putting out 'swhy I was dealing with her – I told them that –

DAD. Why did you decide it was a good idea to start working with her?

BOY. I didn't.

MAN. He didn't.

BOY. Form tutor.

DAD. Form tutor?

BOY. Thought she'd be good for me.

DAD. and?

BOY. I thought she was nuts –

MAN. She had good intentions at heart –

BOY. Intentions to flop my rep –

MAN. Flop your rep?

BOY. Make me look moist.

MAN. Make you look moist?

DAD. I don't get it either.

BOY. Try taming me –

DAD. Taming?

BOY. As if man's an animal –

DAD. My son's not an animal –

MAN. He's not an animal –

DAD. Then why would – he doesn't need taming.

BOY. I know I don't need taming.

MAN. It's not about taming

BOY. It's not about taming – ?

DAD. What's it about?

BOY. what's it about?

MAN. It's about potential –

DAD. Potential doesn't include name-calling –

MAN. No one's name-calling –

BOY. Calling me a hopeless case –

DAD. A hopeless case –

MAN. He's at risk – not yet hopeless –

DAD. This is hopeless –

MAN. This is serious –

BOY. It's always serious –

DAD. It's always serious –

MAN. A serious – offence –

DAD. Allegations –

MAN. It's not an allegation

BOY. I didn't do anything.

MAN. Then what did you do?

DAD. What did you do?

BOY. Nothing – I did nothing.

MAN. Someone did something –

BOY. I told them to stop –

MAN. Who to stop?

BOY. Man dem –

DAD. know yourself?

MAN. Please –

BOY.…She begged them?

MAN. How did it happen?

BOY.…It was after school – around about the time we were
    suppose to meet –

DAD. and?

BOY. and she was waiting for me – near the library –

    I told them where –

MAN. who was it?

BOY. where they could easily sneak up on her – like me – she
    liked that –

DAD. You crept up on her –

BOY. for jokes – trying to be discreet – I get her all the time –
    she don't scream though – I told them –

MAN. They knew what to do –

BOY. They didn't do that though –

DAD. What did they do?

BOY. Two of them walk down the hall – towards her – hooded up – she rolled her eyes – I saw her – she was nervous – they were bate – head down – walking slow – towards her –

MAN. What did they do?

BOY. They walked past her slightly – she relaxed – then they turned and pushed – pulled her – into the girls' toilet –

MAN. So it wasn't the boys' toilets –

BOY. It was the girls' –

DAD. why didn't you go in and stop them?

BOY. I stood back – man dem clawing at her top

MAN. who started it – ?

BOY. I'm not –

DAD. what did you do?

BOY. I did nothing –

MAN. Give me something –

DAD. He did nothing –

MAN. What else happened?

BOY. She scratched one of the man dem – 'bitch' and he punched her – hard

MAN. which one?

BOY. Like I would –

MAN. I – we need to know –

DAD. say what you know –

BOY. They ripped her top – 'her duds are big fam – feel them' – she screamed –

DAD. I don't like this –

MAN. say what you saw –

BOY. Man dem grabbed her shirt – covered her mouth –

DAD. Ain't that enough –

MAN. who was there –

BOY. I ain't about to –

MAN. Just a name –

DAD. don't make him –

BOY. She started crying – struggling – 'hold her, manz' going for the panties

DAD. does he have to – ?

MAN. who was there?

BOY. I ain't about to –

MAN. they won't defend you

DAD. He ain't about to –

BOY. She's trying to squeeze her legs together – she's fighting them – trying to scream for me to help her –

DAD. does he have to – ?

MAN. He needs to –

BOY. Two of them stick their hands between her legs – fingering her – sniffing their fingers – laughing – (*Different voices.*) 'try find the G-spot – yeah – she ain't wet – why ain't she wet'

DAD. He shouldn't – you shouldn't make him –

MAN. I'm not making him –

BOY. She's got her eyes closed – whimpering – One of the man dem is holding her arms so tight – he's giving her burns – 'my turn, fam – let me have a go' he say – 'battery – come we run train on her' – she knows what it means – she squeeze her eyes tight – 'nah, fam, we could be here all night – I've got football practice'

MAN. Football practice – who's that?

BOY. Like man's gonna –

MAN. Oh come on one –

BOY. I lost my voice – I tried to speak – two two's nothing dropped out – just air – breeze – gas – Man dem look at me like don't you want none of this – next man goes – 'he's already been there' –

DAD. That's why she says he was there – he did nothing –

MAN. Did you do nothing?

BOY. we ain't done it – She wanted it to be proper special – I set her up – I did nothing –

MAN. Who else was there?

BOY. I ain't running my mout–

MAN. I put my neck on the line for you –

DAD. What do you want him to say?

MAN. I want him to tell the truth –

BOY. What you think this is joke?

DAD. It's not a joke, boy –

MAN. I don't think it's a joke –

BOY. Don't force me –

MAN. She's in pain –

BOY. I know –

DAD. He knows –

MAN. I'm dealing with this –

DAD. I don't like the way you're –

MAN. You're not helping –

DAD. He's my son –

MAN. She thinks he – he was there –

BOY. She knows – she must know –

MAN. She named you –

DAD. She didn't say he did it –

BOY. Of course I didn't –

MAN. I know – now – you can help – send them down

DAD. Sell them out –

MAN. Give them up –

BOY. No –

MAN. No – ?

BOY. No – I ain't a snitch – snitches get stitches –

DAD. I don't want stitches on my son –

MAN. He won't get –

BOY. I'll be dead

MAN.… You won't die –

BOY. Like you know –

DAD. My son's not dying –

  not at his age –

  not for just any girl –

BOY. She's not any girl –

DAD. I know –

BOY. No you don't know –

MAN. Say something –

BOY. ain't saying nothing –

MAN. Come on – drop me a name – whose – who else was
  there?

DAD. He doesn't want to.

MAN. How do you know what he wants?

DAD. What?

MAN. You don't know him –

DAD. Like you do?

MAN. Maybe – better than you –

DAD. What's that supposed to mean?

MAN. Why don't you let him speak –

DAD. He's already said –

BOY. I can't –

MAN.... Yes you can – You'll be protected –

BOY. By who? – You?

MAN....please... Consider –

BOY. I don't want to

MAN....Dad?

DAD.... You've heard my boy –

MAN....

BOY....

DAD....

Scene Four

BOY. Don't hold my hand –

DAD. Don't hold your hand?

BOY. Yeah – not today –

DAD. Why not?

BOY. I ain't a chick –

DAD. I know you're not a chick –

BOY. Last time –

DAD. Last time?

BOY. Time, you did that, I had to defend it –

DAD. defend it?

BOY. Move up some youts –

DAD. Move up

BOY. Fight them –

DAD. You were fighting?

BOY. I had to –

DAD. Because I held your hand?

BOY. That's like contraband in here –

DAD. Contraband?

BOY. It's illegal –

DAD. I'm your father –

BOY. Yeah, that's legit – but

DAD. But I haven't seen you since –

BOY. Don't shame me –

DAD. Don't shame you?

BOY. Don't shame me

DAD.... Who's shaming who?

BOY. Not in here –

DAD. You care what they think in here –

BOY. Everybody cares what anyone thinks in here –

DAD (*condescending*). Do they think? – What do they think?

BOY. Who?

DAD. In here?

BOY. We're all super bad in here –

DAD. Super bad – ?

BOY. Badder than bad is super bad –

DAD. That's a thing to be?

BOY. In here that's a thing to be –

DAD. Don't get caught up?

BOY. Ain't trying to get caught up –

DAD. But you're in here –

BOY. Just a thing I gotta do –

DAD (*aside*). Just a thing… What you been doing?

BOY. Doing?

DAD. *Doing?* – Eating?

BOY. Don't eat much –

DAD. Don't eat much?

BOY. Food is bad –

DAD. That's not good –

BOY. Nah it's bad –

DAD. You want me to…?

BOY. Nah – I'll firm it.

DAD. Are you sure –

BOY. Certain –

DAD. Certainly look…

BOY. look?

DAD. How are you?

BOY. How am I?

DAD. Yeah… And so big?

BOY. Am I big?

DAD. Bigger –

BOY. Bigger?

DAD. Yes, than before –

BOY. Pushing weights –

DAD. Pushing weights?

BOY. Tryna get stronger –

DAD. You look stronger –

BOY. Do I?

DAD. Yes… well –

BOY. I feel stronger –

DAD. Don't get used to this place –

BOY. I ain't getting used to it –

DAD. I mean it –

BOY. I ain't –

DAD. Doesn't look like it to me –

BOY. Just something to do.

DAD. do what you should do –

BOY. Don't you think I know –

DAD. I don't think you do – It's why you're –

BOY. Dad, don't beg it –

DAD. I'm not one of your –

BOY.…

DAD. I blame myself –

BOY. Blame for what?

DAD. How you've turned out –

BOY. How I've turned out?

DAD. Do you have to be told –

BOY. Told what?

DAD. You have to be told –

BOY. What you telling me –

DAD. I obviously failed –

BOY. failed what?

DAD. Failed you – Your mother –

BOY. She didn't even know my name –

DAD. Shut up –

BOY.…

DAD. What made you like this?

BOY. I made me like this

DAD. Maybe that's the problem –

BOY. It ain't a problem?

DAD. For you maybe, but it's my problem –

BOY.…

DAD.…I can't believe this –

BOY. Have faith –

DAD. faith…

BOY.…You look old –

DAD. Old?

BOY. Older

DAD. Stressed –

BOY. Why you stressing?

DAD. Why do you think?

BOY. It's minor –

DAD. This ain't minor –

BOY. I don't mind –

DAD. I mind – You're just a minor

BOY. That's minor –

DAD. When will you – ?

BOY. Will I what?

DAD. Grow out of this –

BOY. out of what?

DAD. Your behaviour –

BOY. Behaviour?

DAD. Your carefree attitude –

BOY. I don't care – You don't see me free –

DAD. why should you be free?

BOY. Why should I be free?

DAD. The way you go on –

BOY. It's just part of life –

DAD. What life?

BOY. My life –

DAD. Are you thinking about yourself –

BOY. About myself?

DAD. About yourself?

BOY. What's that supposed to mean?

DAD. It means what it is – what is this?

BOY. This is remand –

DAD. remand?

BOY. remand – till court – till sentencing –

DAD. Have you lost your mind?

BOY. I ain't searching for it –

DAD. You should be –

BOY. Why you gassing?

DAD. Shut up –

I'm not your – Know yourself

BOY.…

DAD. They're –

BOY. They're?

DAD. Those boys that did… they're out there –

BOY. Yeah and –

DAD. And you're in here –

BOY. that's right I'm here –

DAD. Rotting –

BOY. I ain't rotting –

DAD. You'll be spoilt –

BOY. how so spoilt?

DAD. Spoilt and discarded –

BOY. Discarded?

DAD. No one will want you –

BOY. Depends on what I want –

DAD. Like you'll have a choice –

BOY. I'll have a choice –

DAD. What be more of a criminal?

BOY. I ain't a criminal –

DAD. Yet –

BOY. why you getting hotted?

DAD. Shut up –

   I'm not your –

BOY.…

DAD. What do you expect to be when –

BOY. depending on how many years –

DAD. How many years?

BOY. Yeah – How many years I get –

DAD. You're looking forward to that –

BOY. I ain't looking forward to it –

DAD. You ain't looking forward to it?

BOY. Why should I look forward to it?

DAD. Then what are you looking forward to?

BOY. I'm looking forward to getting out, man –

DAD. You're looking forward to getting out –

BOY. Yeah… the youts in here –

DAD (*mocking*). The youts in here –

BOY. Youts in here –

DAD. Youts in here?

BOY. Are missing –

DAD. missing?

BOY. cracked up –

DAD. cracked up – taking crack –

BOY. On sumting – On a next thing –

DAD. What next thing?

BOY. next hype –

DAD. hype for what –

BOY. I don't know what – stripes –

DAD. Stripes – ?

BOY. status –

DAD. what status is in here?

BOY. Here – top boy –

DAD. Top of what class –

BOY. No one goes to class –

DAD. They teach you here?

BOY. No one goes to class –

DAD. You go to class –

BOY. I'll be an outcast –

DAD. Be an outcast –

BOY. Outcasts don't last –

DAD. You want to last –

BOY. I want to last –

DAD. Tell a guard –

BOY. They'll want you to grass –

DAD. Grass for what?

BOY. Grass what other boys are doing –

DAD. you can't grass – ?

BOY. Not if I want to last –

DAD. you can't grass –

BOY. I know that –

DAD. that's not what I'm saying –

BOY. Say what you mean then.

DAD.... You know that this can stop now –

BOY. Stop how –

DAD. Tell the truth –

BOY. You know the truth –

DAD. Yes – now let someone else deal with it –

BOY. No need –

DAD. I need it dealt with properly –

BOY. I'm –

DAD. Tell the truth.

BOY.... Tell the truth?

DAD. Just that –

BOY. I didn't do anything –

DAD. That I already know – Tell more – The rest of it –

BOY. I can't do that –

DAD.... You can do that –

BOY. I can't do that –

DAD. Yes you can –

BOY. That's not what's done –

DAD. By who?

BOY. man dem... peeps

DAD. I don't care about peeps –

BOY. You know how difficult – [things would become...]

DAD (*dismissive*). I know –

BOY. If you know –

DAD. Tell the court –

BOY. Tell the court – ?

DAD. Save yourself –

BOY. I'm trying to save myself –

DAD. From what – an easy life –

BOY. Your life isn't easy –

DAD. It's been easier than yours will be –

BOY. Different times –

DAD. Time you start thinking differently –

BOY. I already think differently –

DAD. I don't see how you can say that –

BOY. things will work out –

DAD. work out what you want –

BOY. It will work out –

DAD. No listen to me – You must work it out –

BOY. Yeah I hear you –

DAD. Do you really?

BOY. I'll work it out –

DAD. Do you promise me?

BOY. What's to promise?

DAD. Just say it –

BOY.…

DAD. Say it –

BOY.…Promise

DAD. Yes?

BOY.…Yeah –

End of play.

A Nick Hern Book

Mad About The Boy first published in Great Britain in 2012 as a paperback original by Nick Hern Books Limited, 14 Larden Road, London W3 7ST, in association with Iron Shoes and the Unicorn

Cover photograph: iStockphoto/MissHibiscus
Cover design: Ned Hoste, 2H

Typeset by Nick Hern Books, London
Printed in the UK by Mimeo Ltd, Huntingdon, Cambridgeshire PE29 6XX

A CIP catalogue record for this book is available from the British Library

ISBN 978 1 84842 268 1